Woodwind

Wendy Lynch

Heinemann Library
Chicago, Illinois

Designed by Visual Image
Originated by Dot Gradations
Printed and bound in South China

06 05 04 03 02
10 9 8 7 6 5 4 3

Library of Congress Cataloging-in-Publication Data
Lynch, Wendy, 1945-
    Woodwind / Wendy Lynch.
        p. cm. -- (Musical instruments)
    Includes bibliographical references (p.   ) and index.
    ISBN 1-58810-237-8
    1. Woodwind instruments--Juvenile literature. [1. Woodwind instruments.] I. Title. II. Series.
    ML931 .L96 2001
    788.2'19--dc21

                                                                2001000099

Acknowledgments
The publishers would like to thank the following for permission to reproduce photographs: pp. 4, 5 Pictor; pp. 6, 7 Cumulus/Photodisc; p. 8 Sally Greenhill; p. 9 Clive Sawyer/Pictures; pp. 10, 24, 28, 29 Gareth Boden; p. 11 Photofusion; p. 12 Ray Roberts/Photofusion; p. 13 Bubbles; p. 14 Gareth Boden/JHS & Co.; p. 15 JHS & Co.; p. 16 Franz-Rombout/ Bubbles; p. 17 Odile Noel/Redferns; pp. 18, 25 Rex; p. 19 Chris Stock/Lebrecht collection; p. 20 Michael St. Maur Sheil/Collections; p. 21 Robert Harding; p. 22 Marc Dublin/Travel Ink; p. 23 Corbis; p. 26 All Action; p. 27 Stone.

Cover photograph reproduced with permission of Photodisc.

Special thanks to Susan Lerner for her comments in the preparation of this book.

Every effort has been made to contact copyright holders of any material reproduced in this book. Any omissions will be rectified in subsequent printings if notice is given to the publisher.

Some words are shown in bold, **like this.** You can find out what they mean by looking in the glossary.

Contents

Making Music Together 4

What Are Woodwind Instruments? . .6

The Recorder 8

Making a Sound 10

How the Sound Is Made 12

Types of Recorders 14

Recorder Concerts 16

Types of Woodwinds 18

The Woodwind Family 20

Around the World 22

Famous Music and Musicians 24

Woodwind Music Today 26

Sound Activities 28

Thinking about Woodwinds 30

Glossary 31

More Books to Read 32

Index 32

Making Music Together

There are many musical instruments in the world. Each instrument makes a different sound. We can make music together by playing these instruments in a band or an **orchestra.**

Bands and orchestras are made up of different groups of instruments. One of these groups is called woodwinds. You can see many woodwind instruments in this orchestra.

What Are Woodwind Instruments?

Woodwind instruments get part of their name from the "wind" they need to make a sound. As you blow into them, air pushes against the edge of the **mouthpiece** or **reed.**

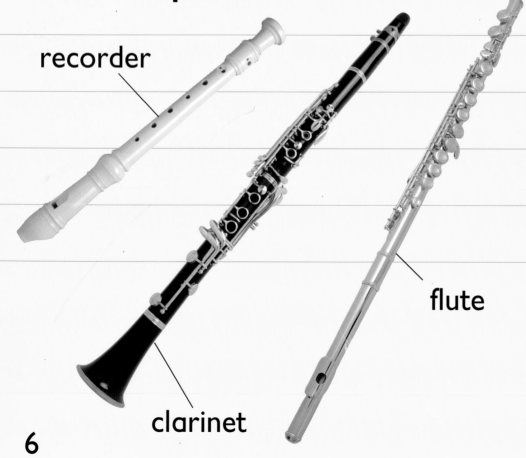

recorder

flute

clarinet

They are also called woodwind instruments because they all used to be made of wood. Now some of them are made of metal or plastic.

bassoon

saxophone

oboe

The Recorder

The recorder is one kind of woodwind instrument. Because it is small and light, it is a popular choice for many schools to teach their students to play.

You can learn to play the recorder with a teacher or use books to help you learn on your own. This boy's book tells how to play different notes and which notes to play to make a tune.

Making a Sound

Most recorders have three parts. The head has a **mouthpiece** that you blow into. The middle has six finger holes and a thumb hole. The foot has a double hole for the little finger.

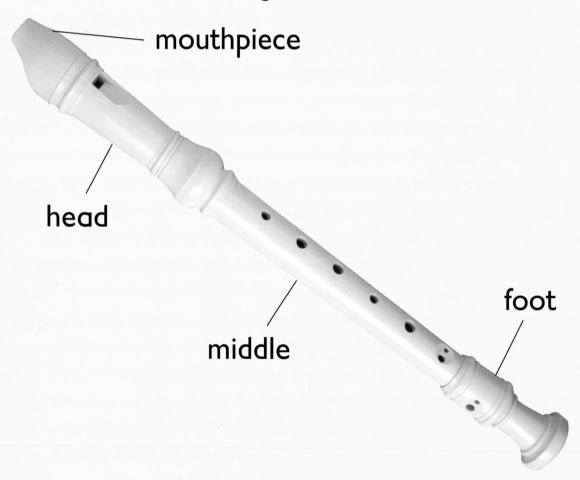

mouthpiece

head

middle

foot

To play the recorder, you blow into the mouthpiece. At the same time, you place your fingers on the finger holes. Covering different holes can make the sound, or **pitch,** higher or lower.

How the Sound Is Made

When you blow into the recorder, you make the air inside the tube move, or **vibrate.** When the air vibrates, it makes a sound.

If you cover the finger holes, you trap more air inside the tube. This makes the air vibrate more slowly, and the **pitch** is lower. If you uncover some or all of the holes, the pitch gets higher.

finger holes

Types of Recorders

There are five sizes of recorders. Bigger ones hold more air and have lower **pitch.** Smaller ones hold less air and sound higher. The soprano recorder is the most popular type used in schools.

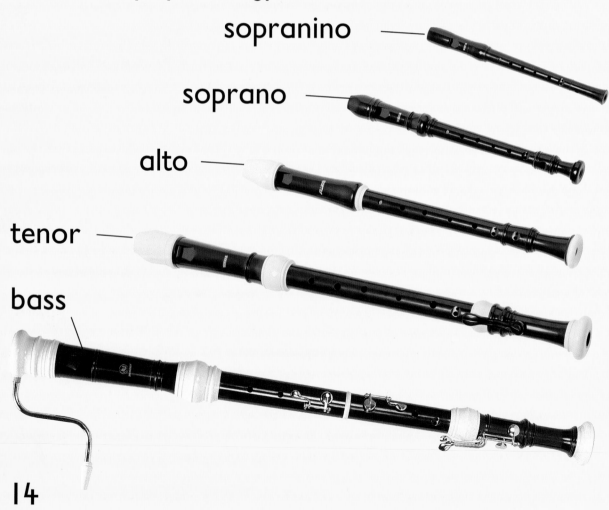

sopranino

soprano

alto

tenor

bass

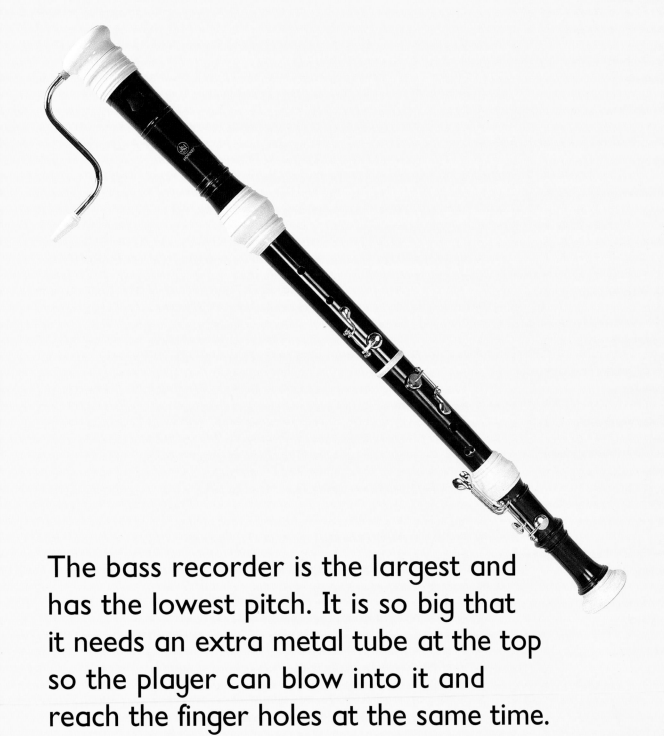

The bass recorder is the largest and has the lowest pitch. It is so big that it needs an extra metal tube at the top so the player can blow into it and reach the finger holes at the same time.

Recorder Concerts

When you play the recorder alone, it is called playing **solo.** You can play songs you know or make up your own music. You can even make bird sounds or play sound games.

You can also play the recorder in a concert with other recorders or with other woodwind instruments. Some **musicians** play recorders in concerts of **Baroque music** from long ago.

Types of Woodwinds

The flute is similar to the recorder, but you blow across a blow hole instead of into a **mouthpiece.** You change the **pitch** by pressing down the keys.

Other woodwinds have a **reed,** made from one or two thin strips of cane, in the mouthpiece. When you blow, the reed **vibrates** against the mouthpiece or against itself, making a sound.

The Woodwind Family

There are other woodwind instruments that make sounds in the same ways. Air inside the tin whistle **vibrates** when you blow into the **mouthpiece.**

Bagpipes are also woodwind instruments. To play the bagpipes, the player blows air into the bag. The player then squeezes the bag, forcing the air into the pipes. This air movement is what makes the sound.

Around the World

You can find woodwind instruments all over the world. The zurna comes from Turkey and is like an oboe. Sometimes people play the zurna at weddings.

The pungi comes from India and is made from a **gourd.** The player blows into one end of the gourd. The sound comes out of two pipes at the other end of the gourd.

Famous Music and Musicians

You can hear woodwind instruments in a concert **orchestra.** In the music *Peter and the Wolf,* the oboe is used for the Duck and the clarinet for the Cat.

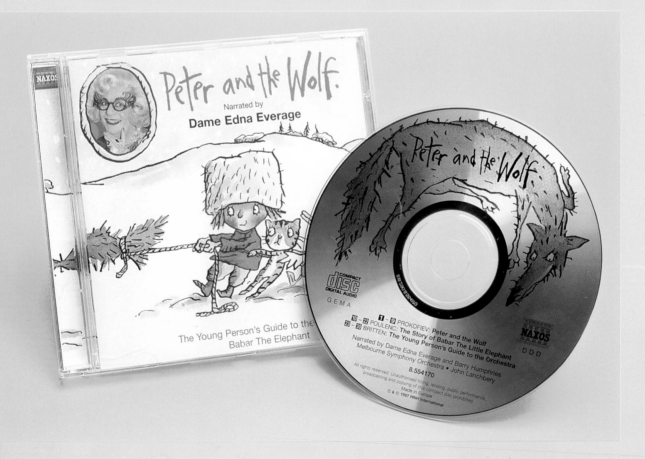

The clarinet and saxophone are also used in **jazz.** Courtney Pine is a famous jazz musician who plays the saxophone.

Woodwind Music Today

Today, you can hear woodwind instruments in **rock, pop, soul,** and **heavy metal** music. The tin whistle is often played in Irish pop and **folk** music.

A **synthesizer** is a keyboard that can **imitate** many different sounds. You can play the sounds of all the woodwind instruments using a synthesizer.

Sound Activities

Pour some water into an empty bottle. Blow across the top to make the air inside **vibrate.** Add some more water and blow again. Does the sound change?

Pick a blade of grass and hold it between your thumbs. Blow between your thumbs. The grass vibrates like a **reed** and makes a sound.

Thinking about Woodwinds

You can find the answers to all of these questions in this book.

1. Why are the instruments in this book called woodwind instruments?

2. What will happen to a woodwind's **pitch** if you cover more finger holes or press more keys?

3. Which kind of recorder is most often used in schools?

4. Which woodwind instruments can you hear in **jazz** music?

5. What is a pungi?

Glossary

Baroque music music written between the years 1600 and 1750

folk traditional style of music from a country or area

gourd large fruit with a hard rind

heavy metal style of loud, energetic rock music with a strong beat

imitate to copy

jazz style of music developed in the United States that is often made up as it is played

mouthpiece part of an instrument placed in or near the mouth

musician person who plays a musical instrument

orchestra large group of musicians who play their musical instruments together

pitch highness or lowness of a sound or musical note

pop popular music

reed thin strip of cane or metal

rock kind of pop music with a strong beat

solo song or piece of music for one person

soul style of music that is full of feeling

synthesizer electronic instrument that can make or change many different sounds

vibrate to move up and down or from side to side very quickly

31

More Books to Read

Harris, Pamela K. *Clarinets*. Chanhassen, Minn.: The Child's World, Incorporated, 2000.

Kalman, Bobbie. *Musical Instruments from A to Z*. New York: Crabtree Publishing Company, 1997.

Turner, Barrie. *Woodwinds & Brass*. North Mankato, Minn.: Smart Apple Media, 1998.

Index

bagpipes 21
bands 4, 5, 26
Baroque music 17
clarinet 24, 25
finger holes 10, 11, 13, 15
flute 7, 18
gourd 23
jazz 25
keys 18
mouthpiece 6, 10, 11, 18, 19, 20
oboe 22, 24
orchestras 4, 5, 24
Peter and the Wolf 24
Pine, Courtney 25

pitch 11, 13, 14, 15, 18
pop music 26
pungi 23
recorder 8–17
  bass recorder 15
  soprano recorder 14
reed 6, 19, 29
rock music 26
saxophone 7, 25
soul music 26
synthesizer 27
tin whistle 20
vibration 12, 13, 19, 20, 28, 29
zurna 22